How to Becom
Tee

From YouTube Beginner to Star Creator!

Amber James

© Copyright 2023-All rights reserved.

The content contained within this book may not be reproduced, duplicated or transmitted without direct written permission from the author or the publisher.

Under no circumstances will any blame or legal responsibility be held against the publisher, or author, for any damages, reparation, or monetary loss due to the information contained within this book, either directly or indirectly.

Legal Notice:
This book is copyright protected. It is only for personal use. You cannot amend, distribute, sell, use, quote or paraphrase any part, or the content within this book, without the consent of the author or publisher.

Disclaimer Notice:
Please note the information contained within this document is for educational and entertainment purposes only.

Table of Contents

Chapter 1: Laying the Groundwork for Your YouTube Journey..................4

Chapter 2: Mastering the Art of Content Creation.11

Chapter 3: Building and Nurturing Your YouTube Community..........21

Chapter 4: Monetizing Your YouTube Channel......29

Chapter 6: Navigating Challenges and Staying Motivated..........48

Chapter 7: Legal and Ethical Considerations for YouTubers..........57

Chapter 8: Building Your Personal Brand as a YouTuber..........67

Chapter 9: Monetizing Your YouTube Channel......76

Chapter 10: Advanced Strategies for Channel Growth and Maintenance..........86

Chapter 1: Laying the Groundwork for Your YouTube Journey

1.1 Introduction

Embarking on a journey to become a YouTuber can be both exciting and overwhelming. YouTube has become one of the most influential platforms, offering a creative space for individuals to share their passions, knowledge, and talents with the world. This chapter will guide you through the essential steps you need to take to lay a solid foundation for your YouTube career. By the end of this chapter, you will have a clear understanding of the fundamentals of becoming a successful YouTuber.

1.2 Define Your Niche and Target Audience

Before you dive into creating content, it's crucial to establish a niche that sets you apart from the crowd. A niche is a specific topic or genre that you are passionate about and knowledgeable in. Choosing a niche will help you create focused content that resonates with your target audience. Some popular niches include gaming, fashion, cooking, technology, and fitness.

Once you have chosen your niche, define your target audience. This will help you tailor your content to the needs and interests of your viewers. For example, if you are creating content about video games, your target audience might be teenagers who love gaming and are looking for tips and reviews.

1.3 Plan Your Content Strategy

A content strategy is a roadmap that outlines the type of content you'll create, your goals, and your posting schedule.

Start by brainstorming content ideas that align with your niche and target audience. You can create a content calendar to help you plan and organize your ideas, ensuring that you have a consistent flow of fresh content.

Set goals for your channel, such as reaching a specific number of subscribers, views, or likes. These goals will help you stay motivated and track your progress. Additionally, establish a posting schedule that works for you, such as uploading videos once or twice a week. Consistency is key, as it helps to build audience loyalty and engagement.

1.4 Create a Compelling Channel Name and Brand Identity

Your channel name is the first impression viewers have of your brand. Choose a name that is unique, memorable, and relevant to your niche. It's essential to keep your channel name consistent across your social media platforms to create a cohesive brand identity.

In addition to your channel name, create a visually appealing channel logo and banner. These elements will help you establish a brand identity that represents your content and appeals to your target audience. You can use design tools like Canva or Adobe Photoshop to create eye-catching graphics.

1.5 Optimize Your Channel for Search and Discoverability

YouTube is the second-largest search engine globally, so optimizing your channel and content for search is crucial for gaining visibility. Start by creating a compelling channel description that includes relevant keywords related to your niche. This will help viewers understand what your channel is about and help YouTube's algorithm recommend your content to the right audience.

Additionally, add relevant tags to your channel, which act as keywords that help YouTube understand your content's context. This will increase the likelihood of your videos appearing in search results and suggested videos.

1.6 Equipment and Software

To create high-quality videos, you'll need some basic equipment and software. While it's possible to start with a smartphone camera, investing in a good-quality camera, microphone, and lighting equipment will significantly improve your video quality. You don't need to break the bank; affordable options are available for budding YouTubers.

For editing your videos, there are various software options available, ranging from free to paid. Some popular choices include iMovie, Adobe Premiere Pro, and Final Cut Pro. Choose a program that fits your budget and skill level, and take the time to learn the ins and outs of your chosen software.

1.7 Collaborate with Other YouTubers

Collaborating with other YouTubers can be a great way to gain exposure and grow your audience. Look for creators within your niche who share similar interests and values. By working together, you can create content that appeals to both of your audiences, potentially increasing your subscriber count and engagement. To initiate a collaboration, reach out to fellow creators through social media or email, and pitch your collaboration idea. Be genuine and respectful, and explain how the collaboration would benefit both parties. You may want to start by collaborating with creators who have a similar audience size to your own, as they may be more open to the opportunity.

1.8 Engage with Your Audience

Building a loyal and engaged audience is crucial for long-term success on YouTube. To do this, make an effort to respond to comments, ask for feedback, and encourage viewers to like, share, and subscribe to your channel. You can also engage with your audience on other social media platforms, such as Instagram, Twitter, and Facebook. This helps you build a stronger connection with your viewers and keeps them invested in your content.

1.9 Track Your Analytics and Adjust Your Strategy

YouTube provides creators with a range of analytics tools to track their channel's performance. Monitor your analytics regularly to identify trends and patterns in your viewers' behavior. This information will help you understand what content resonates with your audience and what areas you may need to improve.

If you notice that certain types of videos perform better than others, consider creating more content in that style. Alternatively, if you find that your audience isn't engaging with a particular type of content, it might be time to pivot or adjust your strategy.

1.10 Be Patient and Persistent

Growing a successful YouTube channel takes time, effort, and dedication. You may not see immediate results, but it's essential to stay persistent and continue refining your content and strategy. Embrace setbacks as learning opportunities and use them to improve your skills and knowledge.

Remember, many successful YouTubers took years to gain traction and build their audience. Stay focused on your goals, and with hard work and determination, you'll be well on your way to becoming a successful YouTuber.

In summary, Chapter 1 provided an overview of the essential steps to lay the groundwork for your YouTube journey. By defining your niche, planning your content strategy, creating a compelling channel name and brand identity, optimizing your channel for search, investing in equipment and software, collaborating with other YouTubers, engaging with your audience, tracking your analytics, and staying patient and persistent, you'll be well-equipped to launch your YouTube channel and begin your journey to success.

Chapter 2: Mastering the Art of Content Creation

2.1 Introduction

In the previous chapter, we discussed the essential steps to lay a solid foundation for your YouTube journey. Now that you have a clear understanding of the fundamentals, it's time to focus on the heart of your channel: your content. This chapter will delve into the various aspects of content creation, including crafting engaging videos, developing your unique style, optimizing your content for search and discoverability, and promoting your videos effectively. By the end of this chapter, you'll have the tools and knowledge to create content that resonates with your target audience and stands out on YouTube.

2.2 Crafting Engaging Videos

To create videos that capture your audience's attention, it's essential to focus on three key aspects: storytelling, visual appeal, and audio quality.

2.2.1 Storytelling

An engaging story is at the core of every successful video. Start by outlining your video's structure, which typically includes an introduction, the main content, and a conclusion. The introduction should grab the viewer's attention and give them a reason to continue watching. The main content should deliver on the promise made in the introduction, providing valuable information, entertainment, or both. Finally, the conclusion should wrap up the video and encourage viewers to take action, such as liking, commenting, or subscribing.

Additionally, make sure your content is relevant to your niche and target audience. Research what your audience is interested in, and try to address their questions, concerns, or pain points in your videos. This will make your content more valuable and appealing to viewers.

2.2.2 Visual Appeal

A visually appealing video will keep viewers engaged and help convey your message effectively. To achieve this, focus on the following elements:

- Composition: Frame your shots to ensure that the subject is in focus and well-positioned within the frame. Utilize the rule of thirds, leading lines, and other composition techniques to create visually pleasing images.
- Lighting: Good lighting is crucial for creating high-quality videos. Invest in affordable lighting equipment, such as softboxes or ring lights, to achieve even, well-lit shots. Experiment with different lighting setups to find what works best for your content.
- Color grading: Color grading can dramatically enhance the look of your videos. Use editing software to adjust the color balance, saturation, and contrast of your footage, creating a cohesive and visually appealing aesthetic.

2.2.3 Audio Quality

Clear and crisp audio is essential for keeping viewers engaged. Invest in a good-quality microphone to ensure that your voice is easy to understand and free of background noise. Additionally, consider adding background music or sound effects to enhance your videos, but make sure they don't overpower your voice or distract from your content.

2.3 Developing Your Unique Style

Standing out on YouTube requires more than just high-quality content. You need to develop a unique style that sets you apart from the competition and resonates with your audience. Consider the following aspects:

- On-camera presence: Cultivate a confident and authentic on-camera presence that reflects your personality. Be genuine and relatable, and strive to make a connection with your viewers. It may take some practice, but your on-camera presence will improve over time.
- Editing style: Your editing style can greatly impact the overall feel of your videos. Experiment with different editing techniques, such as transitions, text overlays, and animations, to create a signature style that is both engaging and reflective of your brand.
- Channel branding: As discussed in Chapter 1, creating a cohesive brand identity is crucial for building recognition and trust with your audience. Ensure that your unique style is consistent across your channel, including your video thumbnails, titles, and descriptions.

2.4 Optimizing Your Content for Search and Discoverability

Now that you have created engaging and visually appealing content, it's crucial to optimize your videos for search and discoverability. This will increase the likelihood of your videos being found by potential viewers and help you grow your audience.

2.4.1 Keyword Research

Identify relevant keywords related to your niche and video topic using keyword research tools such as Google Trends, TubeBuddy, or VidIQ. Incorporate these keywords strategically in your video title, description, and tags to help YouTube's algorithm understand your content and recommend it to the right audience.

2.4.2 Compelling Titles and Thumbnails

Your video title and thumbnail are the first impressions viewers have of your content. To increase click-through rates, create attention-grabbing titles that accurately represent your video's content and include relevant keywords. Avoid using clickbait titles, as they can lead to viewer disappointment and decreased engagement.

Similarly, design eye-catching thumbnails that accurately reflect your video content and entice viewers to click. Use contrasting colors, bold text, and intriguing images to stand out among other videos. Remember to keep your thumbnail style consistent with your channel's branding.

2.4.3 Video Descriptions and Tags

Write detailed video descriptions that provide an overview of your video's content and include relevant keywords. This helps viewers understand what your video is about and helps YouTube's algorithm recommend your content to the right audience.

Additionally, add relevant tags to your videos, which act as keywords that help YouTube understand your content's context. This will increase the likelihood of your videos appearing in search results and suggested videos.

2.5 Promoting Your Videos Effectively

Creating high-quality, optimized content is only half the battle. To grow your audience, you need to actively promote your videos on various platforms.

2.5.1 Social Media Promotion

Share your videos on social media platforms such as Facebook, Twitter, Instagram, and Pinterest to reach a wider audience. Tailor your posts for each platform, and use relevant hashtags to increase visibility. Engage with your followers and encourage them to share your content with their networks.

2.5.2 Collaborations and Cross-Promotions

As discussed in Chapter 1, collaborating with other YouTubers can help you gain exposure and grow your audience. By working together, you can create content that appeals to both of your audiences, potentially increasing your subscriber count and engagement.

You can also reach out to influencers or content creators in your niche for cross-promotions. Offer to share their content on your channel or social media platforms in exchange for them sharing your content with their audience.

2.5.3 Engaging in Communities

Participate in online communities related to your niche, such as forums, Facebook groups, or Reddit threads. Share your videos when appropriate, and engage in meaningful conversations with other members. Be helpful and genuine, rather than overly promotional, to build trust and credibility within the community.

2.5.4 Email Marketing

Create an email list to keep your subscribers informed about your latest videos and news. Encourage viewers to sign up for your newsletter by offering exclusive content, such as behind-the-scenes footage, bonus tips, or early access to new videos.

In summary, Chapter 2 provided a comprehensive guide to mastering the art of content creation. By focusing on crafting engaging videos, developing your unique style, optimizing your content for search and discoverability, and promoting your videos effectively, you'll be well on your way to creating content that resonates with your target audience and stands out on YouTube. As you continue your journey, remember to stay adaptable and open to learning new skills, techniques, and strategies that will help you grow and succeed on the platform.

Chapter 3: Building and Nurturing Your YouTube Community

3.1 Introduction

In the previous chapters, we discussed laying the groundwork for your YouTube journey and mastering the art of content creation. As you create and share engaging content, it's essential to focus on building and nurturing a loyal community of viewers. A strong community can be the driving force behind your channel's growth, as engaged viewers are more likely to interact with your content, share it with others, and contribute to your success. This chapter will guide you through the various aspects of building and nurturing your YouTube community, including fostering engagement, addressing feedback, managing negative comments, and utilizing social media to strengthen your community.

3.2 Fostering Engagement

Viewer engagement is a critical factor in your channel's growth and success. Engaged viewers are more likely to subscribe, like, comment, and share your content, which helps to boost your visibility and attract new viewers. To foster engagement, consider the following strategies:

3.2.1 Encourage Interaction

Invite viewers to interact with your content by asking questions, requesting feedback, or creating polls. This not only increases engagement but also helps you understand your audience's interests and preferences better. Respond to comments and messages in a timely manner, and show appreciation for your viewers' input.

3.2.2 Create Shareable Content

Focus on creating content that viewers will want to share with their friends and followers. This can include entertaining, informative, or inspiring content that resonates with your target audience. Encourage sharing by reminding viewers to share your videos and providing easy-to-use share buttons.

3.2.3 Utilize Calls-to-Action

Include clear calls-to-action (CTAs) in your videos to guide viewers on the desired action, such as subscribing, liking, or leaving a comment. Place CTAs strategically throughout your video, such as in the intro, during the video, and at the end.

3.3 Addressing Feedback and Criticism

As your channel grows, you will inevitably receive feedback and criticism from your viewers. Addressing feedback constructively and using it to improve your content is essential for your channel's growth and development.

3.3.1 Embrace Constructive Criticism

Distinguish between constructive criticism and negative comments. Constructive criticism can provide valuable insights into areas where you can improve your content. Embrace this feedback and use it to refine your skills and techniques.

3.3.2 Acknowledge and Learn from Mistakes

When viewers point out mistakes or inaccuracies in your content, acknowledge them and take steps to correct the issue. This not only demonstrates your commitment to providing accurate and reliable content but also helps to build trust with your audience.

3.4 Managing Negative Comments and Trolls

Dealing with negative comments and trolls can be challenging, but it's important to handle these situations professionally and calmly. Consider the following strategies:

3.4.1 Ignore and Block Trolls

Trolls often seek attention and a reaction from their targets. In most cases, it's best to ignore them and block them from your channel. Engaging with trolls can lead to escalated conflicts and damage your channel's reputation.

3.4.2 Establish and Enforce Community Guidelines

Create clear community guidelines for your channel that outline the acceptable behavior and language in your comment section. Enforce these guidelines by removing comments that violate the rules and banning users who repeatedly engage in harmful behavior.

3.4.3 Focus on Positive Interactions

While it's essential to address negative comments and trolls, don't let them overshadow the positive interactions and support from your loyal viewers. Focus on building relationships with your engaged viewers and fostering a positive, inclusive community.

3.5 Utilizing Social Media to Strengthen Your Community

Social media platforms offer additional opportunities to connect with your audience and strengthen your community. By leveraging these platforms, you can create deeper connections with your viewers and expand your reach. Consider the following strategies:

3.5.1 Create and Share Content Across Platforms

Post exclusive content, such as behind-the-scenes footage, sneak peeks, or updates on your social media platforms. This encourages your YouTube viewers to follow you on other platforms and helps to build a cohesive community across all your online presence.

3.5.2 Engage with Your Audience

Use social media to engage with your audience beyond YouTube. Respond to comments and messages, and participate in conversations relevant to your niche. This shows your viewers that you value their input and are genuinely interested in connecting with them.

3.5.3 Host Giveaways and Contests

Hosting giveaways and contests on your social media platforms can help to boost engagement and attract new followers. Ensure that the giveaway or contest is relevant to your niche and provides value to your audience.

3.5.4 Collaborate with Other Creators and Influencers

Connect with other content creators and influencers in your niche on social media. Share their content, engage in conversations, and collaborate on projects. This can help to grow your audience and strengthen your community by exposing your content to new viewers who share similar interests.

3.6 Organizing and Participating in Live Events

Live events, such as Q&A sessions, live streams, or meet-and-greets, can be an effective way to connect with your audience and build a stronger community. Here are some tips for organizing and participating in live events:

3.6.1 Plan and Promote Your Live Event

Choose a date and time for your live event that works for both you and your audience. Promote the event on your YouTube channel and social media platforms, giving your viewers ample notice to plan for their attendance.

3.6.2 Prepare and Structure Your Live Event

Outline the structure of your live event to ensure that it runs smoothly and maintains viewer interest. Prepare talking points, interactive segments, or demonstrations to keep your audience engaged.

3.6.3 Interact with Your Audience During the Live Event

Encourage viewer participation during the live event by asking questions, soliciting opinions, or requesting feedback. Respond to comments and questions in real-time, and show appreciation for your viewers' input and support.

3.6.4 Utilize Live Events to Support Your Content Strategy

Integrate live events into your overall content strategy by using them to promote new videos, share updates, or address relevant topics in your niche. This can help to strengthen your community by creating a more interactive and dynamic content experience for your viewers.

In summary, Chapter 3 provided an in-depth guide to building and nurturing your YouTube community. By fostering engagement, addressing feedback and criticism, managing negative comments and trolls, utilizing social media to strengthen your community, and organizing and participating in live events, you'll create a loyal and supportive community that contributes to your channel's growth and success. As you continue your YouTube journey, remember that building a strong community takes time and effort, but the rewards are well worth the investment.

Chapter 4: Monetizing Your YouTube Channel

4.1 Introduction

In the previous chapters, we discussed the fundamentals of starting your YouTube journey, mastering content creation, and building a loyal community. As your channel grows and gains traction, you might begin to consider monetization opportunities to generate income from your efforts. This chapter will explore the various methods of monetizing your YouTube channel, including the YouTube Partner Program, brand sponsorships, affiliate marketing, crowdfunding, and selling merchandise. By the end of this chapter, you'll have a comprehensive understanding of the different income streams available to you as a content creator, allowing you to make informed decisions about which monetization strategies best align with your goals and values.

4.2 The YouTube Partner Program

The YouTube Partner Program (YPP) is the platform's primary monetization option, allowing eligible creators to earn revenue through ads displayed on their videos, channel memberships, and Super Chat donations. To qualify for YPP, you must meet the following requirements:

- Have at least 1,000 subscribers
- Have at least 4,000 watch hours in the past 12 months
- Adhere to YouTube's monetization policies, community guidelines, and terms of service

Once you've met these requirements, you can apply for YPP and, if approved, start earning revenue through the following methods:

4.2.1 Ad Revenue

YouTube displays various ad formats, such as display ads, overlay ads, skippable video ads, and non-skippable video ads, on eligible creators' videos. You'll earn revenue based on the number of ad impressions and clicks your videos receive. To maximize your ad revenue, focus on creating engaging, high-quality content that appeals to advertisers and encourages viewers to watch your videos in their entirety.

4.2.2 Channel Memberships

Channel memberships allow your viewers to support your channel financially by paying a monthly fee in exchange for exclusive perks, such as custom badges, emojis, and access to members-only content. This can be an excellent source of recurring revenue and a way to strengthen your community by providing additional value to your most dedicated viewers.

4.2.3 Super Chat and Super Stickers

Super Chat and Super Stickers are features that allow your viewers to make donations during live chat sessions in exchange for highlighted messages or custom stickers. This can be an effective way to generate income during live streams while also encouraging viewer engagement and interaction.

4.3 Brand Sponsorships and Collaborations

Working with brands and sponsors can be a lucrative monetization strategy for established creators with a loyal audience. Brands are often willing to pay creators to promote their products or services in videos, social media posts, or other content. To attract brand sponsorships and collaborations, consider the following tips:

4.3.1 Build a Media Kit

Create a professional media kit that showcases your channel's statistics, demographics, and achievements. This will provide potential sponsors with a clear understanding of your audience, content, and the value you can offer as a creator.

4.3.2 Reach Out to Relevant Brands

Identify brands and companies that align with your niche and target audience, and reach out to them with a well-crafted pitch highlighting the potential benefits of a partnership. Be prepared to negotiate rates and deliverables to ensure a mutually beneficial collaboration.

4.3.3 Maintain Transparency and Authenticity

When promoting sponsored products or services, always disclose the sponsorship to your viewers and maintain your authenticity. Only work with brands and products that you genuinely believe in, as this will help to build trust with your audience and ensure the long-term success of your channel.

4.4 Affiliate Marketing

Affiliate marketing involves promoting products or services in exchange for a commission on any sales generated through your unique affiliate link. This can be an excellent passive income stream for creators, as it allows you to earn revenue without relying solely on YouTube's ad revenue. To get started with affiliate marketing, consider the following steps:

4.4.1 Choose Relevant Affiliate Programs

Research and join affiliate programs that align with your niche and audience interests. Some popular affiliate networks include Amazon Associates, ShareASale, and CJ Affiliate. Additionally, consider partnering with individual companies that offer affiliate programs for their products or services.

4.4.2 Promote Affiliate Products Naturally

Incorporate affiliate products into your content in a natural and authentic way. This can include product reviews, tutorials, or "top 10" lists featuring the products you're promoting. Always disclose your affiliate relationship to your viewers to maintain transparency and trust.

4.4.3 Track and Optimize Your Affiliate Efforts

Monitor your affiliate earnings and analyze the performance of different products and promotion methods. Use this data to optimize your affiliate marketing strategy and focus on the most effective and profitable approaches.

4.5 Crowdfunding

Crowdfunding platforms, such as Patreon, Ko-fi, or Buy Me a Coffee, allow creators to receive financial support directly from their audience in exchange for exclusive content, rewards, or other perks. Crowdfunding can provide a stable and recurring source of income, helping you invest more time and resources into your channel. To launch a successful crowdfunding campaign, consider the following tips:

4.5.1 Choose the Right Platform

Research different crowdfunding platforms to determine which one best aligns with your needs, goals, and audience preferences. Some platforms offer a subscription-based model, while others allow for one-time donations or support.

4.5.2 Offer Valuable Rewards and Perks

Create a tiered reward system that offers valuable and exclusive perks to your supporters. This can include early access to content, behind-the-scenes footage, private live streams, or custom merchandise. Ensure that the rewards you offer provide real value and incentive for your audience to support you financially.

4.5.3 Promote Your Crowdfunding Campaign

Promote your crowdfunding campaign on your YouTube channel and social media platforms, and provide regular updates on your progress and goals. Show appreciation for your supporters by acknowledging their contributions and keeping them informed about how their support impacts your content and channel.

4.6 Selling Merchandise

Selling custom merchandise, such as t-shirts, hoodies, hats, or accessories, can be an effective way to generate income while also promoting your channel and brand. To successfully sell merchandise, consider the following steps:

4.6.1 Design High-Quality and Unique Products

Create unique, high-quality designs that resonate with your audience and represent your channel's brand. Consider collaborating with a professional designer if necessary to ensure your merchandise is visually appealing and well-designed.

4.6.2 Choose a Reliable Print-On-Demand Service

Partner with a reliable print-on-demand service, such as Printful, Teespring, or Spreadshirt, to handle product creation, shipping, and customer service. This will allow you to focus on creating content and promoting your merchandise without worrying about logistics.

4.6.3 Promote Your Merchandise Effectively

Feature your merchandise in your videos and social media posts, and encourage your viewers to support your channel by purchasing your products. Offer limited-time discounts or promotions to incentivize sales and generate interest in your merchandise.

In summary, Chapter 4 provided a comprehensive guide to monetizing your YouTube channel through various methods, including the YouTube Partner Program, brand sponsorships, affiliate marketing, crowdfunding, and selling merchandise. By exploring and implementing these monetization strategies, you can generate income from your content creation efforts and invest in your channel's growth and success. As you embark on your monetization journey, remember to prioritize transparency, authenticity, and providing value to your audience, as these factors will ultimately determine the long-term success and sustainability of your income streams.

Chapter 5: Scaling and Expanding Your YouTube Presence

5.1 Introduction

As your YouTube channel grows and you successfully monetize your efforts, it's essential to think about how to scale and expand your presence to maintain momentum and achieve continued success. In this chapter, we'll explore strategies for scaling your content production, maintaining consistency, leveraging analytics, and expanding your online presence beyond YouTube. By implementing these strategies, you'll be better equipped to maximize your channel's growth potential and adapt to the ever-evolving landscape of online content creation.

5.2 Scaling Your Content Production

Scaling your content production is critical for maintaining growth and keeping your audience engaged. As your channel becomes more successful, you may need to produce more content or invest in higher production quality to meet your audience's expectations. Consider the following strategies for scaling your content production:

5.2.1 Develop a Content Pipeline

Create a content pipeline that allows you to plan, produce, and schedule your videos efficiently. This can include brainstorming and researching new video ideas, outlining scripts or storyboards, filming and editing content, and uploading and optimizing your videos. By streamlining your content production process, you'll be better equipped to maintain a consistent upload schedule and manage the increased workload as your channel grows.

5.2.2 Outsource and Delegate Tasks

As your channel expands, you may need to outsource or delegate certain tasks to maintain efficiency and focus on your core strengths as a creator. This can include hiring a video editor, collaborating with other creators, or working with a social media manager. Delegating tasks can help you focus on content creation and strategy while ensuring that other aspects of your channel are managed effectively.

5.2.3 Invest in Quality Equipment and Resources

As you generate more revenue from your channel, consider reinvesting in better equipment, software, and resources to improve the quality of your content. This can include upgrading your camera, investing in better lighting or audio equipment, or purchasing premium editing software. Improved production quality can help to attract and retain viewers and showcase your professionalism as a creator.

5.3 Maintaining Consistency

Consistency is a key factor in maintaining audience engagement and ensuring the long-term success of your channel. As you scale your content production, it's essential to maintain a consistent upload schedule, tone, and branding. Here are some tips for maintaining consistency:

5.3.1 Establish a Regular Upload Schedule

Develop a regular upload schedule that aligns with your content production capabilities and audience preferences. Communicate your schedule to your viewers and strive to meet their expectations by uploading new content consistently.

5.3.2 Maintain a Consistent Tone and Branding

Ensure that your content, visuals, and messaging maintain a consistent tone and branding that reflects your channel's niche and target audience. This helps to create a cohesive experience for your viewers and strengthens your channel's identity.

5.3.3 Adapt and Evolve While Maintaining Consistency

As your channel grows and evolves, be prepared to adapt your content strategy and production techniques to stay relevant and meet your audience's changing interests. However, ensure that any changes align with your channel's core identity and maintain consistency with your existing content.

5.4 Leveraging Analytics for Growth

As you scale and expand your YouTube presence, it's crucial to leverage analytics to understand your channel's performance, identify opportunities for growth, and make data-driven decisions. YouTube Analytics provides valuable insights into your audience, engagement, and revenue, which can help to inform your content strategy and optimize your efforts. Consider the following tips for leveraging analytics:

5.4.1 Monitor Key Performance Metrics

Track key performance metrics, such as views, watch time, audience retention, and subscriber growth, to gain insights into your channel's performance and identify trends or areas for improvement. Regularly reviewing these metrics can help you make informed decisions about your content strategy and production techniques.

5.4.2 Analyze Audience Demographics and Interests

Understand your audience's demographics, interests, and preferences by analyzing data on age, gender, location, and viewing habits. Use this information to tailor your content and targeting strategies to better serve your audience and attract new viewers.

5.4.3 Optimize Your Content for Discoverability

Use analytics data to identify keywords, topics, and formats that perform well in terms of search and discovery. Optimize your video titles, descriptions, tags, and thumbnails to increase the likelihood of your content being discovered by new viewers and improving your search rankings.

5.4.4 Test and Iterate Your Content Strategy

Leverage analytics data to test different content formats, topics, and promotional strategies, and measure their impact on your channel's performance. Use these insights to iterate and refine your content strategy, focusing on the approaches that yield the best results.

5.5 Expanding Your Online Presence Beyond YouTube

As your YouTube channel grows, it's essential to consider expanding your online presence beyond the platform to diversify your income streams, strengthen your community, and increase your overall reach. Consider the following strategies for expanding your online presence:

5.5.1 Launch a Website or Blog

Create a website or blog to showcase your content, provide additional information about your channel, and offer resources or services relevant to your niche. A website or blog can serve as a central hub for your online presence and provide additional opportunities for monetization, such as display advertising, sponsored content, or selling digital products.

5.5.2 Utilize Other Social Media Platforms

Leverage other social media platforms, such as Instagram, Twitter, TikTok, or Facebook, to connect with your audience, share content, and promote your YouTube channel. Diversifying your online presence can help you reach new audiences, strengthen your community, and provide additional avenues for monetization and growth.

5.5.3 Explore Podcasting

Consider launching a podcast to share your expertise, insights, and opinions on topics relevant to your niche. Podcasting can help you connect with your audience in a more intimate and personal way and provide additional opportunities for monetization, such as sponsored content or affiliate marketing.

5.5.4 Collaborate with Creators on Other Platforms

Partner with creators on other platforms, such as Twitch streamers, bloggers, or Instagram influencers, to expand your reach and tap into new audiences. Collaborations can help to strengthen your online presence, diversify your content offerings, and foster relationships with like-minded creators.

In summary, Chapter 5 provided a comprehensive guide to scaling and expanding your YouTube presence to maintain momentum and achieve continued success. By focusing on scaling your content production, maintaining consistency, leveraging analytics, and expanding your online presence beyond YouTube, you'll be better equipped to maximize your channel's growth potential and adapt to the ever-evolving landscape of online content creation. As you continue your YouTube journey, remember that growth and expansion require ongoing effort, adaptation, and a commitment to providing value to your audience. With persistence, creativity, and a data-driven approach, you can achieve lasting success as a content creator.

Chapter 6: Navigating Challenges and Staying Motivated

6.1 Introduction

As you progress on your YouTube journey, you will inevitably encounter challenges, setbacks, and moments of doubt. It's essential to learn how to navigate these challenges and maintain the motivation to persevere and continue creating content. In this chapter, we'll discuss common challenges faced by YouTubers, strategies for overcoming these obstacles, and tips for staying motivated and maintaining a healthy work-life balance. By the end of this chapter, you'll be better prepared to face the challenges that come with being a content creator and maintain the drive and passion needed for long-term success.

6.2 Common Challenges Faced by YouTubers

Every content creator's journey is unique, but there are some common challenges that many YouTubers face. By understanding these challenges, you can better prepare yourself to navigate them and develop resilience in your YouTube career.

6.2.1 Dealing with Criticism and Negative Feedback

As a YouTuber, you'll likely encounter negative feedback and criticism from viewers or other creators. This can be difficult to handle, particularly when comments are harsh or unconstructive. Learning how to manage criticism and use it as an opportunity for growth is crucial to maintaining your motivation and self-confidence.

6.2.2 Managing Algorithm Changes and Platform Policies

YouTube's algorithms and policies are continually evolving, which can affect your channel's visibility and performance. Adapting to these changes and finding ways to maintain or improve your channel's performance is an ongoing challenge for many creators.

6.2.3 Balancing Content Creation with Personal Life

Creating and maintaining a YouTube channel can be time-consuming and demanding, particularly as your channel grows and your audience's expectations increase. Balancing your content creation efforts with your personal life, relationships, and self-care is essential for maintaining your well-being and preventing burnout.

6.2.4 Navigating Monetization Challenges

As you monetize your channel, you may face challenges related to fluctuating ad revenue, brand sponsorship negotiations, or changes in YouTube's monetization policies. Navigating these challenges and developing diverse income streams is critical for maintaining financial stability and ensuring the long-term success of your channel.

6.3 Strategies for Overcoming Challenges

Facing challenges is an inevitable part of being a YouTuber, but by developing effective coping strategies, you can overcome obstacles and maintain your motivation to continue creating content. Consider the following strategies for overcoming common challenges:

6.3.1 Handling Criticism and Negative Feedback

- Develop a thick skin: Understand that not everyone will like your content, and some viewers may leave negative comments. Focus on the positive feedback and constructive criticism, and try not to take unconstructive negativity personally.
- Use criticism as an opportunity for growth: Consider whether there is any truth or value in the criticism you receive, and use it as an opportunity to improve your content and grow as a creator.
- Engage with your supportive community: Focus on the positive relationships and connections you've built with your audience, and remember

that your content resonates with and brings value to many viewers.

6.3.2 Adapting to Algorithm Changes and Platform Policies

- Stay informed: Keep up-to-date with YouTube's algorithm changes and platform policies by following industry news, YouTube Creator Studio updates, and other sources of information.
- Experiment and adapt: Test different content formats, topics, and promotion strategies to see what works best under the current algorithm and policies. Be prepared to adapt your content strategy as needed to maintain or improve your channel's performance.
- Diversify your online presence: Expand your online presence beyond YouTube, as discussed in Chapter 5, to mitigate the impact of potential algorithm changes or policy updates on your overall online visibility and income streams.

6.3.3 Balancing Content Creation with Personal Life

- Establish a routine: Develop a consistent routine for creating, editing, and uploading content, and allocate specific times for work and personal activities. This can help you maintain a healthy balance between your YouTube career and your personal life.
- Set boundaries: Clearly communicate your work hours and boundaries to friends and family, and prioritize self-care and personal relationships during your designated personal time.

- Learn to delegate: As mentioned in Chapter 5, consider outsourcing or delegating certain tasks to help manage your workload and maintain a healthy balance between your YouTube career and personal life.

6.3.4 Navigating Monetization Challenges

- Diversify your income streams: Develop multiple income streams, as discussed in Chapter 4, to reduce your reliance on any single source of revenue and mitigate the impact of fluctuations in ad revenue or changes in monetization policies.
- Stay informed about industry trends and best practices: Keep up-to-date with industry news, best practices, and strategies for monetizing your channel, and be prepared to adapt your monetization efforts as needed.
- Develop a financial safety net: Save a portion of your earnings to create a financial safety net, which can help you navigate periods of fluctuating income or unexpected challenges.

6.4 Staying Motivated and Maintaining a Healthy Work-Life Balance

Maintaining your motivation and passion for content creation is crucial for achieving long-term success as a YouTuber. The following tips can help you stay motivated, avoid burnout, and maintain a healthy work-life balance:

6.4.1 Set Realistic Goals and Celebrate Achievements

Establish realistic goals for your channel's growth, content production, and monetization efforts, and regularly assess your progress towards these goals. Celebrate your achievements, both big and small, and use them as motivation to continue working towards your long-term objectives.

6.4.2 Connect with Your Audience and Other Creators

Engage with your audience regularly through comments, social media, and livestreams to build connections, receive feedback, and maintain motivation. Additionally, network with other content creators to share experiences, advice, and support, and collaborate on projects to maintain your passion and creativity.

6.4.3 Prioritize Self-Care and Mental Health

Ensure that you allocate time for self-care, relaxation, and hobbies outside of content creation. This can include exercise, meditation, spending time with friends and family, or pursuing personal interests. Prioritizing your mental health and well-being is crucial for maintaining your motivation and preventing burnout.

6.4.4 Embrace Change and Adaptability

Recognize that your YouTube journey will involve change, growth, and adaptation. Embrace these changes and view them as opportunities for personal and professional development. Maintaining a flexible and adaptable mindset can help you stay motivated and resilient in the face of challenges and setbacks.

In summary, Chapter 6 provided a comprehensive guide to navigating the challenges and setbacks that come with being a YouTube content creator and maintaining the motivation and passion needed for long-term success. By understanding common challenges, developing strategies for overcoming obstacles, and prioritizing your mental health and work-life balance, you can cultivate the resilience and adaptability needed to thrive in the ever-evolving world of YouTube. As you continue on your YouTube journey, remember that setbacks and challenges are a natural part of the process, and with perseverance, dedication, and a growth mindset, you can achieve lasting success as a content creator.

Chapter 7: Legal and Ethical Considerations for YouTubers

7.1 Introduction

As a YouTube content creator, it's essential to understand the legal and ethical considerations that come with your work. Being aware of these factors and conducting your channel in a responsible and compliant manner can help you avoid potential legal issues, maintain your reputation, and foster a positive and inclusive community. In this chapter, we'll discuss important legal and ethical considerations for YouTubers, including copyright and fair use, privacy and data protection, disclosure of affiliate and sponsored content, and promoting a positive online environment. By the end of this chapter, you'll be better equipped to navigate the complex landscape of legal and ethical issues surrounding YouTube content creation.

7.2 Copyright and Fair Use

Understanding copyright law and fair use principles is crucial for avoiding potential legal disputes and protecting your own creative works. The following sections provide an overview of these concepts and offer guidance on how to navigate them as a YouTube content creator:

7.2.1 Copyright Basics

Copyright is a legal concept that grants creators the exclusive right to control the use, reproduction, and distribution of their original creative works, such as music, videos, photographs, and written content. As a YouTuber, you must ensure that you have the necessary permissions or licenses to use copyrighted materials in your videos.

7.2.2 Fair Use

Fair use is a doctrine in U.S. copyright law that allows for the limited use of copyrighted material without obtaining permission from the copyright holder. Fair use typically applies in cases of criticism, comment, news reporting, teaching, scholarship, or research. To determine whether your use of copyrighted material falls under fair use, consider the following four factors:

1. Purpose and character of the use: Transformative uses, such as parodies or critiques, are more likely to be considered fair use.
2. Nature of the copyrighted work: Factual or non-fiction works are more likely to be subject to fair use than creative or fictional works.
3. Amount and substantiality of the portion used: Using smaller portions of the copyrighted work and avoiding the use of the "heart" of the work increases the likelihood of fair use.
4. Effect of the use on the potential market for or value of the copyrighted work: If your use of the copyrighted material does not negatively impact the market for the original work, it may be more likely to be considered fair use.

Please note that fair use laws can vary by country, and it's important to research and understand the specific laws applicable in your jurisdiction.

7.2.3 Navigating Copyright and Fair Use on YouTube

To avoid potential copyright disputes and protect your channel, consider the following tips:

- Use royalty-free or licensed music: Many websites offer royalty-free music or music licensed under a Creative Commons license that you can use in your videos. Alternatively, you can create your own original music or collaborate with musicians to create custom tracks for your content.
- Obtain permissions or licenses: If you wish to use copyrighted materials in your videos, ensure that you obtain the necessary permissions or licenses from the copyright holder.
- Apply fair use principles: If you believe that your use of copyrighted material falls under fair use, ensure that you understand and apply the four factors outlined above. Be aware that fair use is a complex and subjective area of law, and it's wise to consult a legal professional if you're unsure about your specific situation.

7.3 Privacy and Data Protection

As a YouTuber, it's important to respect the privacy of individuals featured in your videos and comply with relevant data protection laws, such as the General Data Protection Regulation (GDPR) in the European Union or the California Consumer Privacy Act (CCPA) in the United States. To navigate privacy and data protection concerns, consider thefollowing guidelines:

7.3.1 Respect Personal Privacy

- Obtain consent: When filming individuals, particularly in private settings, ensure that you have their permission to include them in your videos. This

is especially important when featuring minors or individuals who may be in vulnerable situations.
- Be mindful of sensitive information: Avoid sharing personal or sensitive information about others, such as contact details, home addresses, or financial information, without their explicit consent.
- Respect requests for privacy: If someone requests that their image or information be removed from your video, seriously consider their request and take appropriate action, keeping in mind the potential legal and ethical implications.

7.3.2 Comply with Data Protection Laws

- Be transparent: Clearly inform your audience about the types of personal information you collect, how it's used, and the measures in place to protect their privacy. This information can be communicated through a privacy policy on your website or in your video descriptions.
- Obtain consent for data collection: If you collect personal information from your viewers, such as email addresses for a newsletter or personal details for a contest, ensure that you obtain their consent and provide them with the option to opt-out of future communications.
- Implement security measures: Take appropriate steps to protect the personal information you collect, such as using secure storage systems, encryption, and strong passwords.

7.4 Disclosure of Affiliate and Sponsored Content

Being transparent about affiliate and sponsored content is not only an ethical best practice but also a legal requirement in many jurisdictions. The Federal Trade Commission (FTC) in the United States, for example, mandates that creators clearly disclose their relationships with brands when promoting products or services. To ensure compliance with these guidelines, consider the following tips:

- Clearly disclose sponsored content: If a brand sponsors your video or provides you with free products for review, clearly disclose this relationship to your audience. This can be done by verbally stating the sponsorship in your video or including a written disclosure in the video description or overlay text.
- Use appropriate disclaimers for affiliate links: If you include affiliate links in your video description, ensure that you disclose your relationship with the affiliate program and inform your audience that you may receive a commission if they make a purchase through your link.
- Be honest and transparent: When promoting products or services, provide your honest opinion and be transparent about any potential biases or incentives that may influence your recommendations.

7.5 Promoting a Positive Online Environment

As a content creator, you have a responsibility to foster a positive and inclusive online environment for your audience. By promoting respect, empathy, and open dialogue, you can create a welcoming community and contribute to a healthier digital landscape. Consider the following guidelines:

- Model respectful behavior: Treat others with kindness and respect, both in your videos and your interactions with your audience. Avoid engaging in or promoting cyberbullying, harassment, or hate speech.
- Encourage constructive feedback and open dialogue: Foster a community where viewers feel comfortable sharing their opinions and engaging in constructive discussions. Encourage your audience to express their thoughts and feedback in a respectful manner.
- Address negative behavior: If you notice toxic or harmful behavior within your community, address it promptly and take appropriate action, such as removing offensive comments or blocking individuals who repeatedly engage in harmful behavior.

In summary, Chapter 7 provided a comprehensive guide to the legal and ethical considerations that YouTubers must navigate in their content creation journey. By understanding and adhering to copyright and fair use principles, respecting personal privacy and data protection laws, disclosing affiliate and sponsored content, and promoting a positive online environment, you can conduct your YouTube channel in a responsible and compliant manner. As you continue to grow as a content creator, remember that ethical and legal considerations are an essential part of your work, and by prioritizing these aspects, you can maintain your reputation, protect your channel, and foster a positive community that supports your long-term success.

7.6 Conclusion

As your YouTube channel grows and evolves, it's crucial to maintain a strong foundation of legal and ethical knowledge and practices. By staying informed about relevant laws and guidelines and conducting your channel in a responsible and transparent manner, you can avoid potential legal disputes, maintain your credibility, and contribute to a healthier digital landscape.

As a content creator, you have the power to influence the lives of your viewers and the broader online community. By prioritizing legal and ethical considerations in your work, you can use this influence for good, creating content that not only entertains and educates but also fosters a positive and inclusive environment for your audience.

As you continue on your YouTube journey, keep these legal and ethical guidelines in mind and strive to be a responsible and conscientious creator. By doing so, you'll be better equipped to navigate the complex world of YouTube content creation and achieve lasting success in your career.

Chapter 8: Building Your Personal Brand as a YouTuber

8.1 Introduction

Establishing a strong personal brand is essential for any aspiring YouTuber looking to stand out in the highly competitive online landscape. A well-crafted personal brand not only helps you build a loyal audience but also opens up opportunities for partnerships, collaborations, and monetization. In this chapter, we'll guide you through the process of building your personal brand, including identifying your unique selling proposition, creating a consistent visual identity, leveraging social media platforms, and engaging in strategic networking. By the end of this chapter, you'll be equipped with the knowledge and tools to create a personal brand that sets you apart and supports your long-term success on YouTube.

8.2 Identifying Your Unique Selling Proposition

Your unique selling proposition (USP) is the factor that distinguishes you from other content creators and makes your channel special. Identifying your USP is the first step in building a strong personal brand. To determine your USP, consider the following questions:

- What is your niche or area of expertise? What specific topics or subjects do you cover in your videos?
- What is your content style? Are your videos informational, entertaining, inspiring, or a combination of these elements?
- What unique experiences, skills, or perspectives do you bring to your content? How do these factors set you apart from other creators in your niche?

Once you've identified your USP, ensure that it's consistently communicated through your content, channel branding, and interactions with your audience. This will help you build a cohesive personal brand that resonates with your target viewers.

8.3 Creating a Consistent Visual Identity

A consistent visual identity is essential for creating a recognizable and memorable personal brand. Your visual identity includes elements such as your logo, channel banner, video thumbnails, color palette, and typography. To create a consistent visual identity, consider the following tips:

8.3.1 Design a Professional Logo

Your logo is the visual representation of your personal brand and should be distinctive, memorable, and reflective of your USP. Consider working with a professional graphic designer or using online design tools to create a high-quality logo that captures the essence of your channel.

8.3.2 Develop a Cohesive Channel Banner

Your channel banner is the first visual element that viewers see when they visit your YouTube page. Design a banner that incorporates your logo, color palette, and typography, and reflects your USP and content style. Ensure that your banner is visually appealing and optimized for display on various devices.

8.3.3 Create Eye-Catching Video Thumbnails

Video thumbnails are a crucial aspect of your visual identity, as they can significantly impact your click-through rate and overall channel performance. Design custom thumbnails that are visually consistent with your logo, color palette, and typography, and feature engaging images or text that entice viewers to click on your videos.

8.3.4 Establish a Consistent Color Palette and Typography

Choose a color palette and typography that reflects your personal brand and use these elements consistently throughout your visual identity. This includes your logo, channel banner, video thumbnails, and any other visual elements associated with your channel. Consistency in color and typography helps reinforce your brand identity and makes your content easily recognizable to your audience.

8.4 Leveraging Social Media Platforms

Social media platforms are a powerful tool for expanding your reach, building your personal brand, and connecting with your audience beyond YouTube. By maintaining an active presence on relevant social media platforms, you can showcase different aspects of your personality, share behind-the-scenes content, and engage with your audience in a more personal and authentic manner. Consider the following tips for leveraging social media platforms to strengthen your personal brand:

8.4.1 Choose the Right Platforms

Identify the social media platforms that are most relevant to your target audience and content niche. Focus on a few platforms where you can maintain a consistent and engaging presence, rather than spreading yourself too thin across multiple platforms. Some popular platforms to consider include Instagram, Twitter, Facebook, TikTok, and LinkedIn.

8.4.2 Create Platform-Specific Content

Tailor your content to the specific platform you are using, taking into account the platform's unique features and audience preferences. For example, share short video clips or behind-the-scenes content on Instagram Stories, post thought-provoking questions or polls on Twitter, or share longer-form written content on LinkedIn.

8.4.3 Maintain a Consistent Brand Identity

Ensure that your visual identity, messaging, and USP are consistent across all your social media profiles. This includes using your logo and color palette, maintaining a consistent tone and voice in your posts, and sharing content that aligns with your personal brand and YouTube channel.

8.4.4 Engage with Your Audience

Social media platforms provide an opportunity for you to interact with your audience and build a strong, loyal community. Respond to comments, ask for feedback, and engage in conversations with your followers to create a sense of connection and trust.

8.5 Strategic Networking

Building relationships with fellow content creators, industry professionals, and influencers can help you expand your network, increase your visibility, and strengthen your personal brand. Engaging in strategic networking can lead to opportunities for collaborations, partnerships, and cross-promotion. Consider the following networking tips:

8.5.1 Attend Industry Events and Conferences

Attending industry events, conferences, and meetups can help you connect with like-minded individuals, learn from industry experts, and gain valuable insights into emerging trends and best practices. Make an effort to network with fellow content creators and professionals in your niche, and be open to potential collaboration opportunities.

8.5.2 Engage in Online Communities

Participate in relevant online communities, such as forums, Facebook groups, and subreddit communities, to share your expertise, learn from others, and establish your credibility as a thought leader in your niche. Engage in meaningful conversations, provide valuable insights, and support others in the community.

8.5.3 Collaborate with Fellow Creators and Influencers

Collaborating with fellow content creators and influencers can help you expand your audience, showcase your expertise, and strengthen your personal brand. Identify potential collaboration partners who share similar values, interests, and target audiences, and propose mutually beneficial projects or initiatives.

8.6 Conclusion

Building a strong personal brand is an ongoing process that requires consistent effort, strategic planning, and a focus on delivering value to your audience. By identifying your unique selling proposition, creating a consistent visual identity, leveraging social media platforms, and engaging in strategic networking, you can establish a personal brand that sets you apart from the competition and supports your long-term success on YouTube.

As you continue to grow and evolve as a content creator, remember to regularly reassess your personal brand and make any necessary adjustments to ensure that it remains relevant, authentic, and reflective of your unique strengths and passions. By doing so, you'll be well-positioned to forge meaningful connections with your audience, create impactful content, and achieve lasting success in the ever-changing world of YouTube.

Chapter 9: Monetizing Your YouTube Channel

9.1 Introduction

As your YouTube channel grows and gains traction, it's important to consider how you can monetize your content and generate revenue from your efforts. Monetizing your channel not only helps you support yourself financially but also enables you to invest in the growth and development of your channel. In this chapter, we'll explore various monetization strategies for YouTubers, including YouTube's Partner Program, sponsored content, affiliate marketing, merchandise sales, and crowdfunding. By the end of this chapter, you'll have a comprehensive understanding of the different revenue streams available to you and how to effectively implement them to maximize your earnings as a content creator.

9.2 YouTube Partner Program

The YouTube Partner Program (YPP) is the primary monetization platform for creators on YouTube. Through the YPP, you can earn revenue from ads displayed on your videos, YouTube Premium subscriptions, and other revenue-generating features, such as Super Chat and Channel Memberships. To be eligible for the YPP, you must meet the following requirements:

- Your channel must have at least 1,000 subscribers

- You must have at least 4,000 watch hours in the past 12 months
- You must comply with YouTube's monetization policies, including copyright and community guidelines

Once you meet the eligibility requirements, you can apply to the YouTube Partner Program and start earning revenue from your content. It's important to note that your earnings may vary based on factors such as your audience demographics, video watch time, and advertiser demand.

9.2.1 Understanding Ad Revenue

Ad revenue is the primary source of income for most creators in the YouTube Partner Program. YouTube displays ads on your videos, and you earn a share of the revenue generated from these ads. There are several types of ads that can appear on your videos, including display ads, overlay ads, skippable video ads, non-skippable video ads, and sponsored cards. To maximize your ad revenue, consider the following tips:

- Create engaging, high-quality content that keeps viewers watching for longer periods of time. This will increase your watch time and make your videos more attractive to advertisers.
- Target your content to a specific audience or demographic that is appealing to advertisers. This can help you secure higher-paying ads and boost your overall revenue.
- Regularly review your YouTube Analytics to understand which types of content generate the

highest ad revenue and adjust your content strategy accordingly.

9.2.2 Leveraging YouTube Premium

YouTube Premium is a subscription service that offers ad-free viewing, access to YouTube Originals, and other premium features. As a YouTube Partner, you can earn a share of the revenue generated from YouTube Premium subscribers who watch your content. The more watch time your videos receive from Premium subscribers, the greater your share of the revenue.

9.2.3 Utilizing Channel Memberships, Super Chat, and Super Stickers

Channel Memberships, Super Chat, and Super Stickers are additional revenue-generating features available to YouTube Partners. With Channel Memberships, viewers can pay a monthly fee to receive exclusive perks, such as custom badges, emojis, and access to members-only content. Super Chat and Super Stickers allow viewers to make one-time payments to have their messages or stickers prominently displayed during live chat events.

To maximize your earnings from these features, consider offering exclusive perks, engaging with your audience during live events, and regularly promoting your membership program and live chat opportunities.

9.3 Sponsored Content

Partnering with brands to create sponsored content is another effective monetization strategy for YouTubers. Sponsored content involves promoting a product or service in your videos in exchange for payment from the sponsoring company. To successfully secure sponsorships, consider the following tips:

- Establish a strong personal brand and target audience. Brands are more likely to partner with creators who have a well-defined niche and a loyal, engaged following.
- Reach out to companies and brands that align with your content niche and audience interests. This will increase the likelihood of securing sponsorships and ensure that your sponsored content is relevant and engaging for your viewers.
- Be transparent about sponsored content by disclosing any paid partnerships in accordance with FTC guidelines and YouTube's ad policies. This will help maintain your credibility and trust with your audience.

When negotiating sponsored content deals, consider factors such as your channel size, engagement rate, and audience demographics to determine your pricing. Remember to always prioritize the value and relevance of your sponsored content for your viewers, as excessive or poorly-executed sponsorships can negatively impact your audience's perception of your channel.

9.4 Affiliate Marketing

Affiliate marketing involves promoting products or services in your videos and earning a commission for each sale made through your unique referral link. This monetization strategy can be an effective way to generate passive income, as you continue to earn commissions long after your videos have been published. To get started with affiliate marketing, follow these steps:

- Sign up for affiliate programs that align with your content niche and audience interests. Some popular affiliate networks include Amazon Associates, ShareASale, and CJ Affiliate.
- Promote products or services in your videos in a genuine and authentic manner, sharing your personal experiences and insights to provide value to your viewers.
- Include your affiliate links in your video descriptions and encourage your viewers to use them when making purchases. Be transparent about your affiliate partnerships and disclose any affiliate links in accordance with FTC guidelines.

To maximize your earnings from affiliate marketing, focus on promoting high-quality products or services that resonate with your audience and offer value beyond the commission you receive.

9.5 Merchandise Sales

Selling merchandise, such as apparel, accessories, or other branded items, is another popular monetization strategy for YouTubers. Merchandise sales not only generate revenue but also help to strengthen your personal brand and foster a sense of community among your viewers. To launch a successful merchandise line, consider the following tips:

- Develop a unique, high-quality product range that reflects your personal brand and appeals to your target audience.
- Partner with a reputable merchandise provider, such as Teespring, Printful, or Spreadshirt, to handle the production, fulfillment, and customer service aspects of your merchandise sales.
- Promote your merchandise in your videos and across your social media platforms, incorporating it into your content in a natural and engaging way.

To maximize your merchandise sales, consider offering exclusive or limited-edition items, running promotions or discounts, and seeking feedback from your audience to continually improve and expand your product range.

9.6 Crowdfunding

Crowdfunding platforms, such as Patreon and Ko-fi, allow your audience to financially support your content creation through one-time donations or recurring monthly contributions. In exchange for their support, you can offer your patrons exclusive perks, such as early access to videos, behind-the-scenes content, or the ability to influence your content decisions. To effectively leverage crowdfunding as a monetization strategy, consider the following tips:

- Clearly communicate the benefits of supporting your content creation and the value your patrons will receive in exchange for their contributions.
- Offer a range of tiered rewards to accommodate different levels of financial support, ensuring that your perks are enticing and valuable for your patrons.
- Maintain regular communication with your patrons through updates, exclusive content, and direct interactions to foster a sense of connection and appreciation for their support.

9.7 Conclusion

Monetizing your YouTube channel is an essential aspect of building a sustainable and rewarding career as a content creator. By exploring various monetization strategies, such as the YouTube Partner Program, sponsored content, affiliate marketing, merchandise sales, and crowdfunding, you can diversify your income sources and maximize your earning potential. As you implement these strategies, remember to prioritize the value and relevance of your content for your viewers, as maintaining a loyal and engaged audience is the key to long-term success on YouTube.

As your channel grows and evolves, continually assess your monetization strategies and make adjustments as needed to optimize your revenue streams. Stay informed about industry trends, emerging platforms, and new monetization opportunities to ensure that you're staying ahead of the curve and maximizing your potential as a content creator. By doing so, you'll be well-positioned to turn your passion for creating YouTube content into a rewarding and sustainable career.

In the next chapter, we'll explore advanced strategies for growing and maintaining your YouTube channel, including leveraging analytics, conducting regular channel audits, and adapting to changes in the YouTube ecosystem. With these advanced strategies in your toolkit, you'll be better equipped to navigate the ever-changing world of YouTube and achieve lasting success as a content creator.

Chapter 10: Advanced Strategies for Channel Growth and Maintenance

10.1 Introduction

In the previous chapters, we've covered the fundamentals of starting and growing a YouTube channel, building a personal brand, and monetizing your content. As you continue to develop your channel and gain experience as a content creator, it's important to implement advanced strategies to further grow your audience, optimize your content, and maintain your channel's success. In this chapter, we'll delve into advanced tactics for YouTube channel growth and maintenance, including leveraging YouTube Analytics, conducting regular channel audits, adapting to changes in the YouTube ecosystem, and staying informed about industry trends and best practices. By the end of this chapter, you'll be equipped with a comprehensive toolkit of advanced strategies to help you navigate the ever-changing world of YouTube and achieve lasting success as a content creator.

10.2 Leveraging YouTube Analytics

YouTube Analytics is a powerful tool that provides you with valuable insights into your channel's performance, audience engagement, and content effectiveness. By regularly reviewing your analytics data and applying these insights to your content strategy, you can make data-driven decisions to optimize your channel's growth and success. In this section, we'll explore key YouTube Analytics metrics and how to use them to inform your content strategy.

10.2.1 Key Metrics

Some of the most important metrics to monitor in YouTube Analytics include:

- Watch Time: The total amount of time viewers have spent watching your videos. Watch time is a critical metric for YouTube's algorithm, as it indicates the level of audience engagement with your content.
- Average View Duration: The average length of time viewers watch your videos. This metric can help you assess whether your content is holding viewers' attention and identify opportunities to improve audience retention.
- Impressions: The number of times your video thumbnails are shown to viewers on YouTube. Impressions can provide insight into the effectiveness of your video titles and thumbnails in attracting viewer interest.
- Click-Through Rate (CTR): The percentage of impressions that result in a video view. A higher CTR indicates that your video titles and

thumbnails are effectively capturing viewer attention and encouraging them to watch your content.
- Audience Demographics: Information about the age, gender, and geographic location of your viewers. Understanding your audience demographics can help you tailor your content to better resonate with your target audience and attract advertisers.
- Traffic Sources: The various sources through which viewers are finding your videos, such as search, suggested videos, or external websites. Analyzing your traffic sources can help you identify effective methods for promoting your content and reaching new audiences.

10.2.2 Using Analytics to Inform Your Content Strategy

Regularly reviewing your YouTube Analytics data can help you identify trends, patterns, and opportunities for improvement in your content strategy. Consider the following tips for using analytics insights to optimize your channel:

- Identify your top-performing videos and analyze the factors that contributed to their success, such as engaging topics, effective video structure, or strong audience retention. Apply these insights to future videos to replicate and build upon this success.
- Analyze your audience retention data to identify points in your videos where viewers tend to drop off. Adjust your video structure, pacing, or

content to better hold viewer attention and increase watch time.
- Monitor your traffic sources to identify effective methods for reaching new audiences and promoting your content. Consider focusing on these methods or exploring new promotional strategies to further expand your reach.
- Use your audience demographics data to tailor your content to better resonate with your target audience. This may include adjusting your language, tone, or cultural references to better connect with your viewers.

10.3 Conducting Regular Channel Audits

A channel audit is a comprehensive evaluation of your YouTube channel's performance, content, and overall strategy. Regularly conducting channel audits can help you identify areas for improvement, optimize your content for audience engagement, and ensure that your channel remains on track to achieve its goals. Consider the following steps for conducting a thorough channel audit:

10.3.1 Review Your Channel's Performance Metrics

Start by reviewing your channel's key performance metrics in YouTube Analytics, such as watch time, average view duration, impressions, CTR, audience demographics, and traffic sources. Identify any areas of concern or opportunities for improvement and develop a plan to address these issues in your content strategy.

10.3.2 Evaluate Your Content Strategy

Assess your content strategy to determine whether it aligns with your channel's goals and target audience. Consider the following questions:

- Are your videos consistently delivering value to your audience?
- Do your video topics align with your channel's niche and target audience interests?
- Are you effectively leveraging trends and current events in your content?

Based on your evaluation, make any necessary adjustments to your content strategy to better serve your audience and achieve your channel's objectives.

10.3.3 Assess Your Channel's Branding and Presentation

Examine your channel's overall branding and presentation, including your channel name, logo, banner, video thumbnails, and descriptions. Ensure that your branding is cohesive, professional, and effectively communicates your channel's value proposition to potential viewers.

10.3.4 Review Your Video Optimization Techniques

Evaluate your video optimization practices, such as your keyword research, video titles, descriptions, tags, and thumbnail design. Identify any areas for improvement and implement changes to optimize your videos for discoverability and audience engagement.

10.3.5 Analyze Your Audience Engagement

Assess your audience engagement efforts, including your responsiveness to comments, participation in live chat events, and interaction with your viewers on social media platforms. Determine whether your engagement strategies are effectively fostering a sense of community and connection with your audience.

10.3.6 Identify Areas for Improvement and Set New Goals

Based on your channel audit findings, identify any areas for improvement and develop a plan to address these issues. Set new goals for your channel's growth, performance, and content quality, and regularly monitor your progress towards these goals.

10.4 Adapting to Changes in the YouTube Ecosystem

The YouTube ecosystem is constantly evolving, with changes in audience preferences, platform features, and industry trends. As a content creator, it's essential to stay informed about these changes and adapt your content strategy accordingly. Consider the following tips for staying ahead of the curve in the ever-changing world of YouTube:

- Regularly monitor industry news, updates, and best practices to stay informed about emerging trends, platform changes, and new opportunities for growth.
- Participate in YouTube creator communities, such as online forums, social media groups, and

networking events, to exchange ideas, insights, and experiences with fellow creators.
- Continuously experiment with new content formats, video styles, and promotional techniques to keep your content fresh and engaging for your audience.
- Be prepared to pivot your content strategy in response to changing audience preferences or platform features, while maintaining your channel's core focus and value proposition.

10.5 Staying Informed About Industry Trends and Best Practices

In addition to adapting to changes in the YouTube ecosystem, staying informed about industry trends and best practices can help you maintain a competitive edge as a content creator. Consider the following resources and strategies for staying up-to-date on the latest developments in the YouTube creator community:

- Subscribe to industry newsletters, blogs, and podcasts that focus on YouTube content creation, platform updates, and creator success stories.
- Follow prominent creators, YouTube experts, and industry influencers on social media platforms to stay informed about their insights, experiences, and advice.
- Attend industry conferences, workshops, and networking events to learn from other creators, expand your professional network, and stay informed about the latest trends and best practices.

Conclusion

In this chapter, we've explored advanced strategies for YouTube channel growth and maintenance, including leveraging YouTube Analytics, conducting regular channel audits, adapting to changes in the YouTube ecosystem, and staying informed about industry trends and best practices. By implementing these strategies, you can effectively navigate the ever-changing world of YouTube and ensure the long-term success of your channel.

As you continue to develop your skills and experience as a content creator, remember that the key to achieving lasting success on YouTube is to consistently create high-quality, engaging content that delivers value to your audience. Focus on honing your craft, experimenting with new ideas, and learning from your experiences to continually improve your content and grow your audience.

Moreover, as a content creator, it's important to maintain a healthy work-life balance and prevent burnout by setting realistic goals, prioritizing self-care, and seeking support from your network of fellow creators, friends, and family. Building a successful YouTube channel is a marathon, not a sprint, and maintaining your well-being and passion for content creation is essential for sustained success.

In conclusion, by applying the strategies and insights shared throughout this book, you'll be well on your way to building a thriving YouTube channel and achieving your goals as a content creator. Remember to stay true to your personal brand, continuously learn and adapt, and, most importantly, enjoy the journey of creating content and connecting with your audience. Best of luck on your YouTube journey!

What Did You Think?

First of all, thank you for purchasing this book. We know you could have picked any number of books to read, but you picked this book and for that, we are extremely grateful.

If you enjoyed this book and found some benefit in reading this, we'd love to hear from you and hope that you could take some time to post a review on Amazon. Your feedback and support will help us to know what you like.

You can do this by going to your orders on Amazon and selecting the book and then reviewing it.

Once again, thank you!

Printed in Great Britain
by Amazon